Adult Coloring Book

Mythical Images:

Intricate, out-of-the-box designs in a fantasy adult coloring book for relaxation and stress relief

By: O.O. Linton

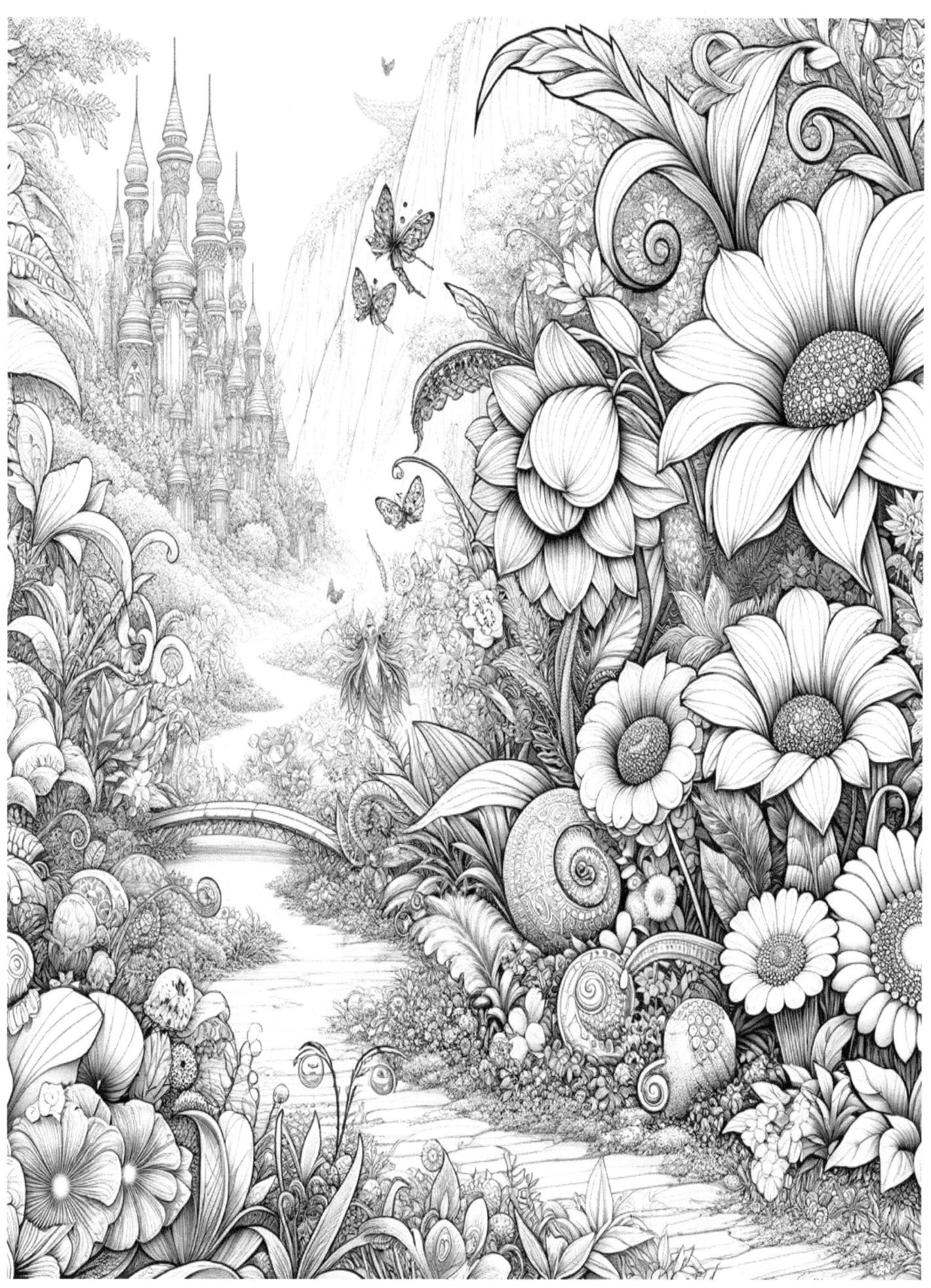

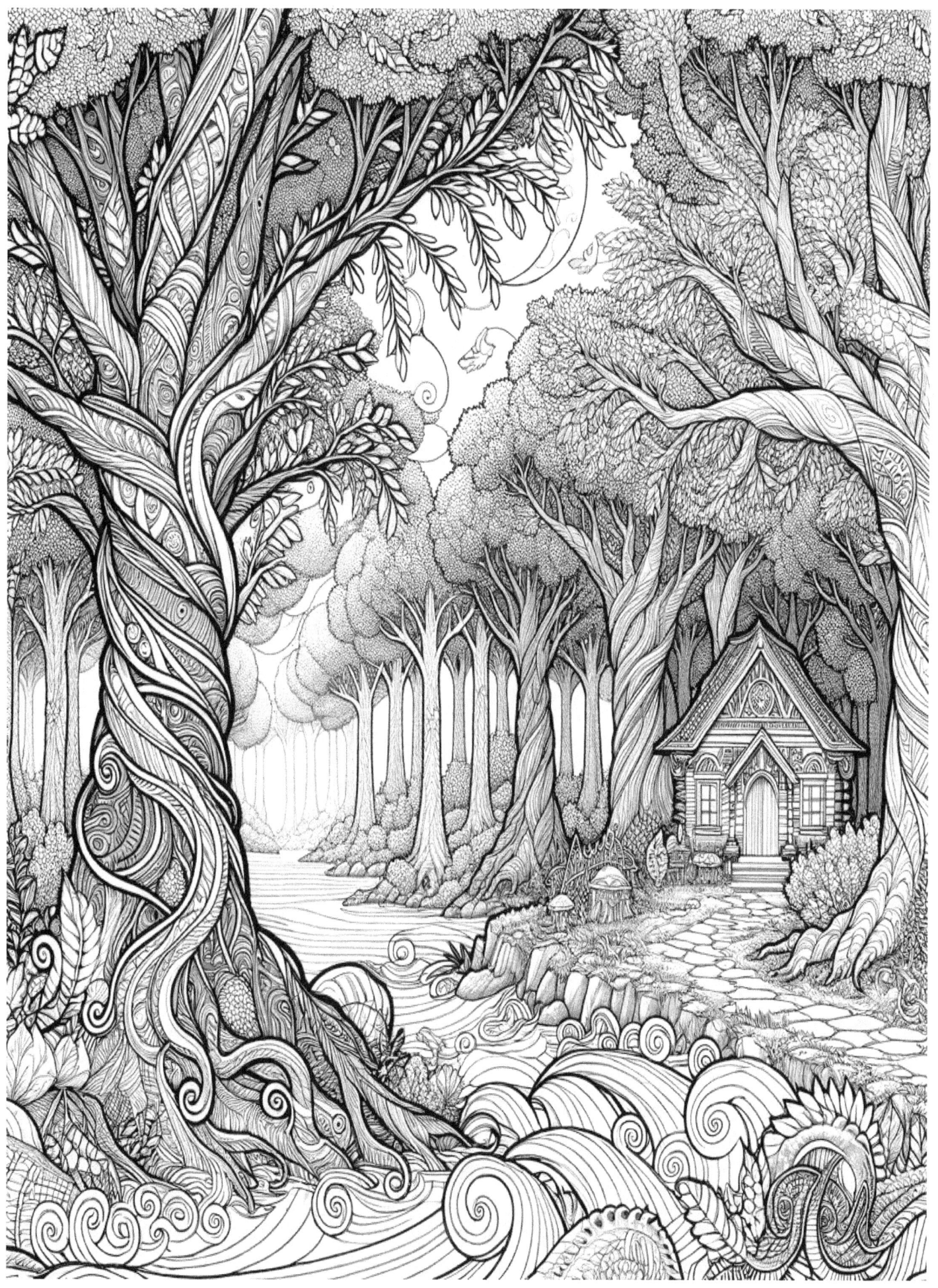

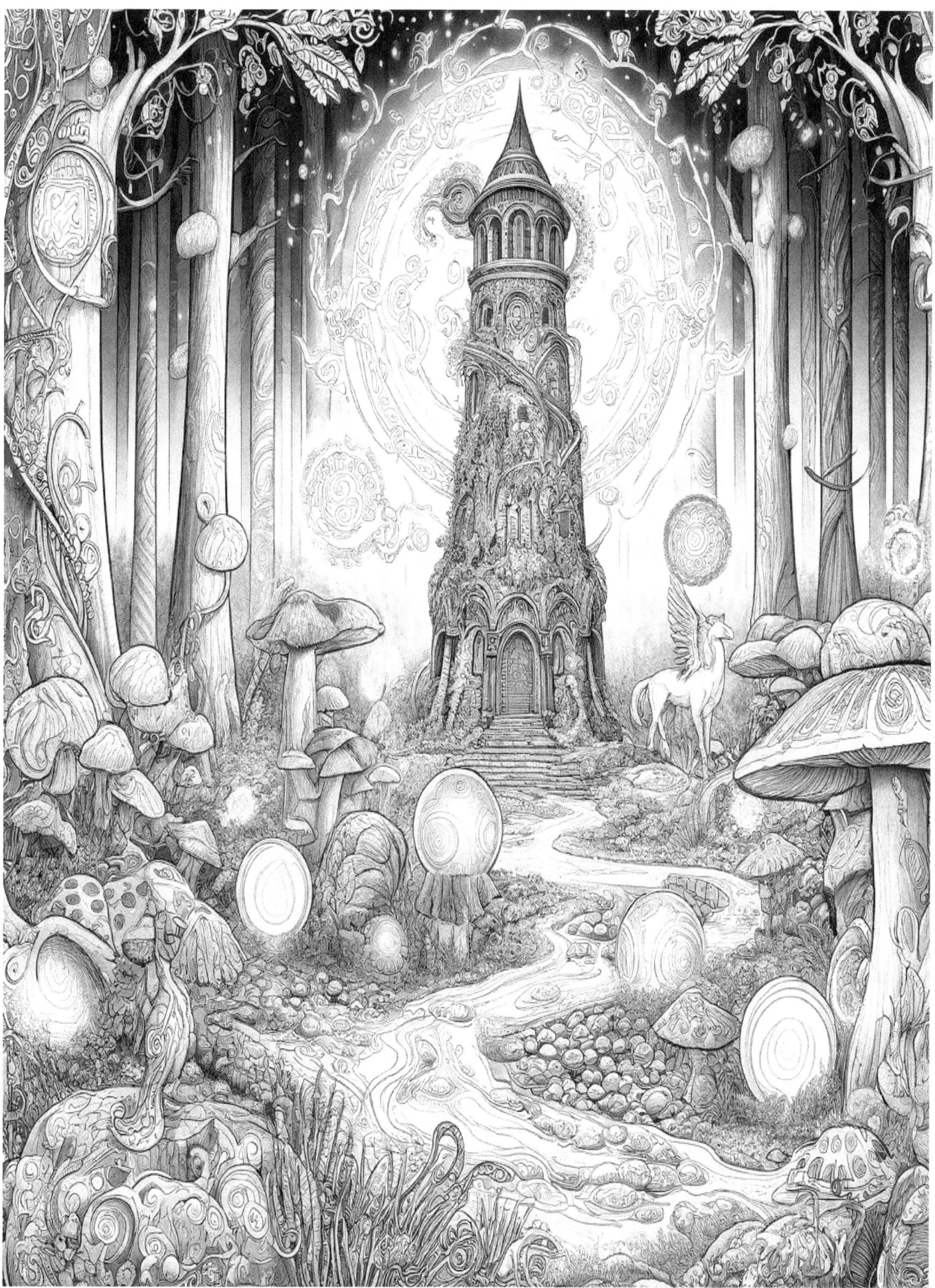

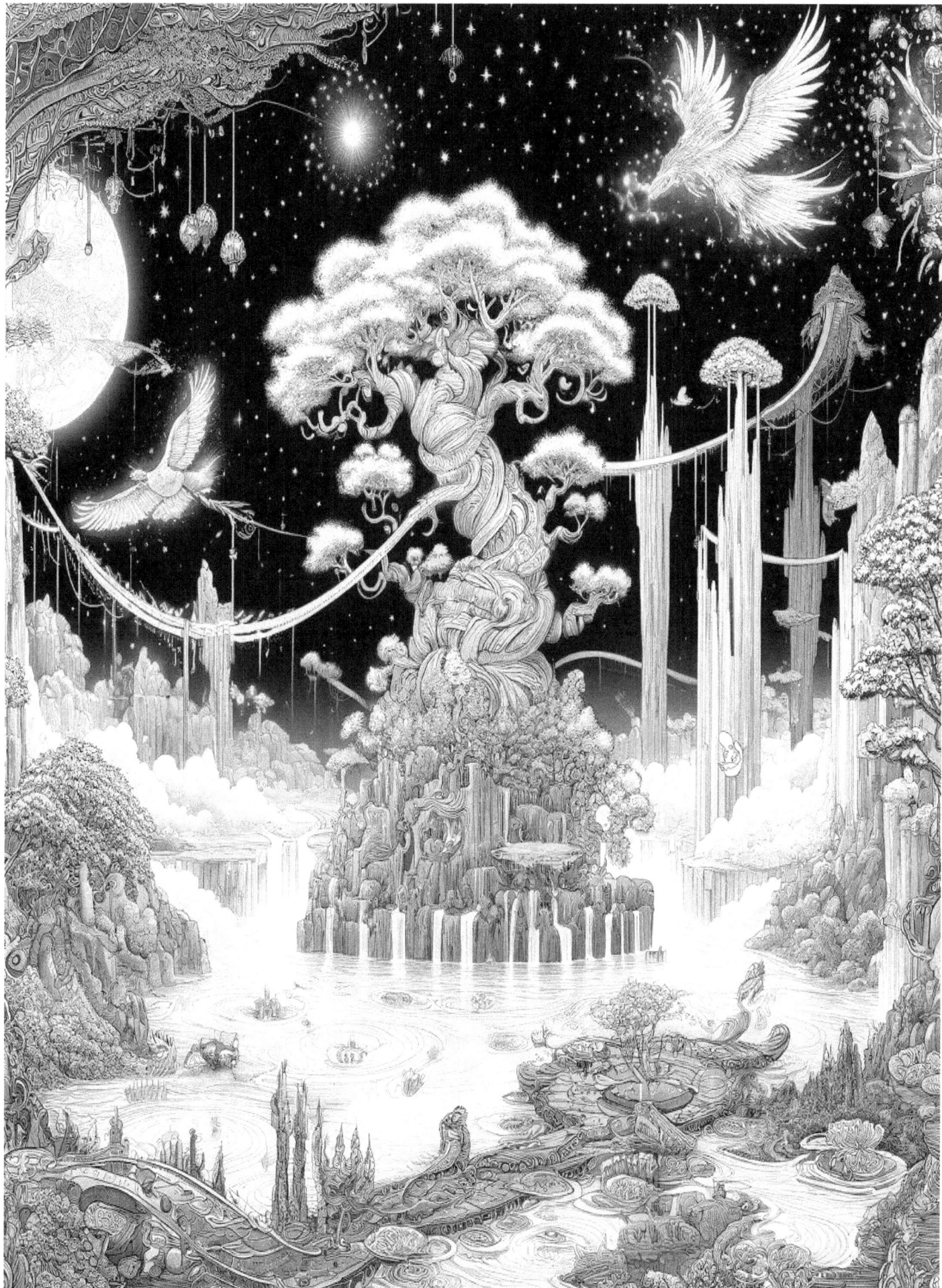

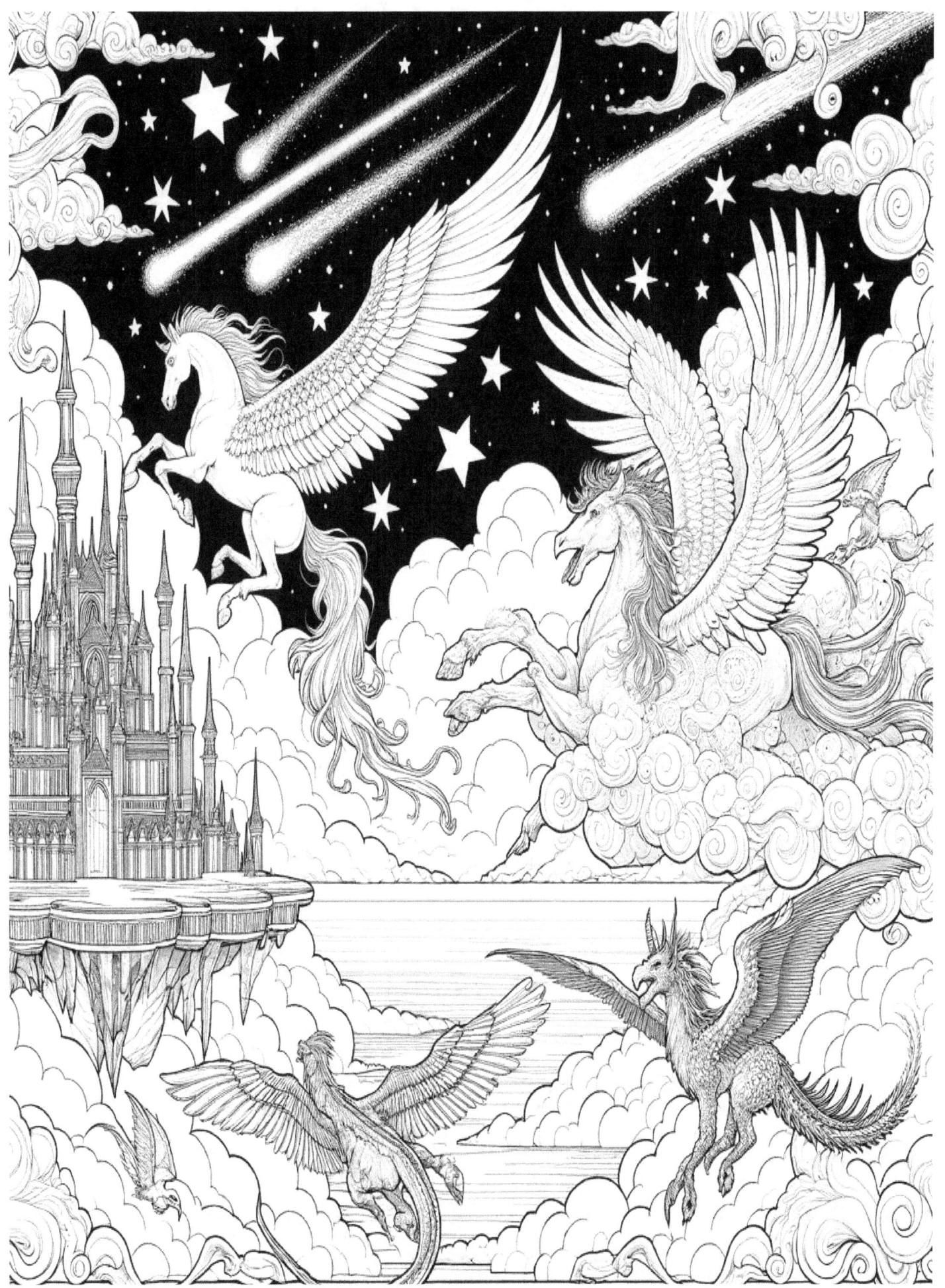

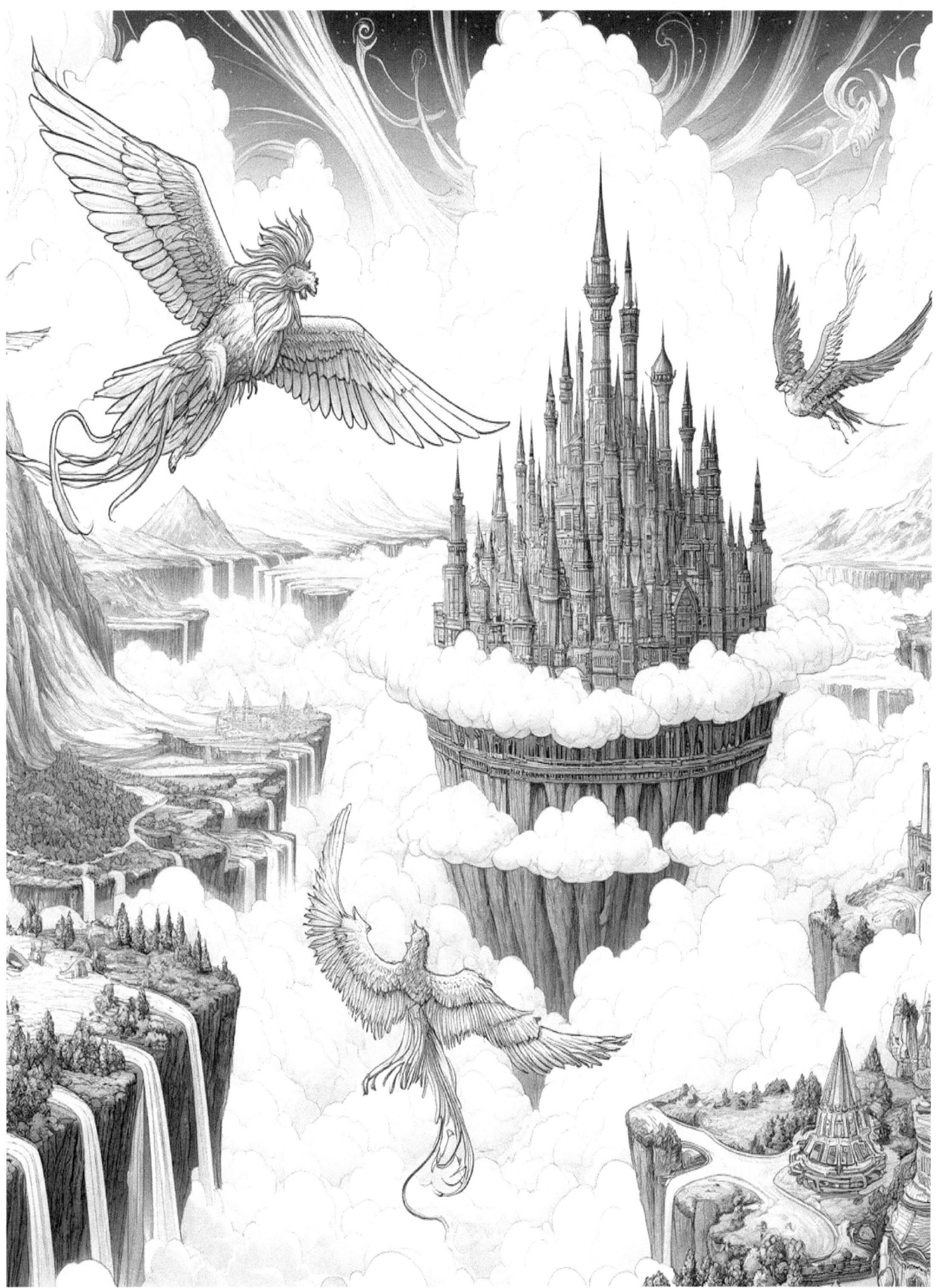

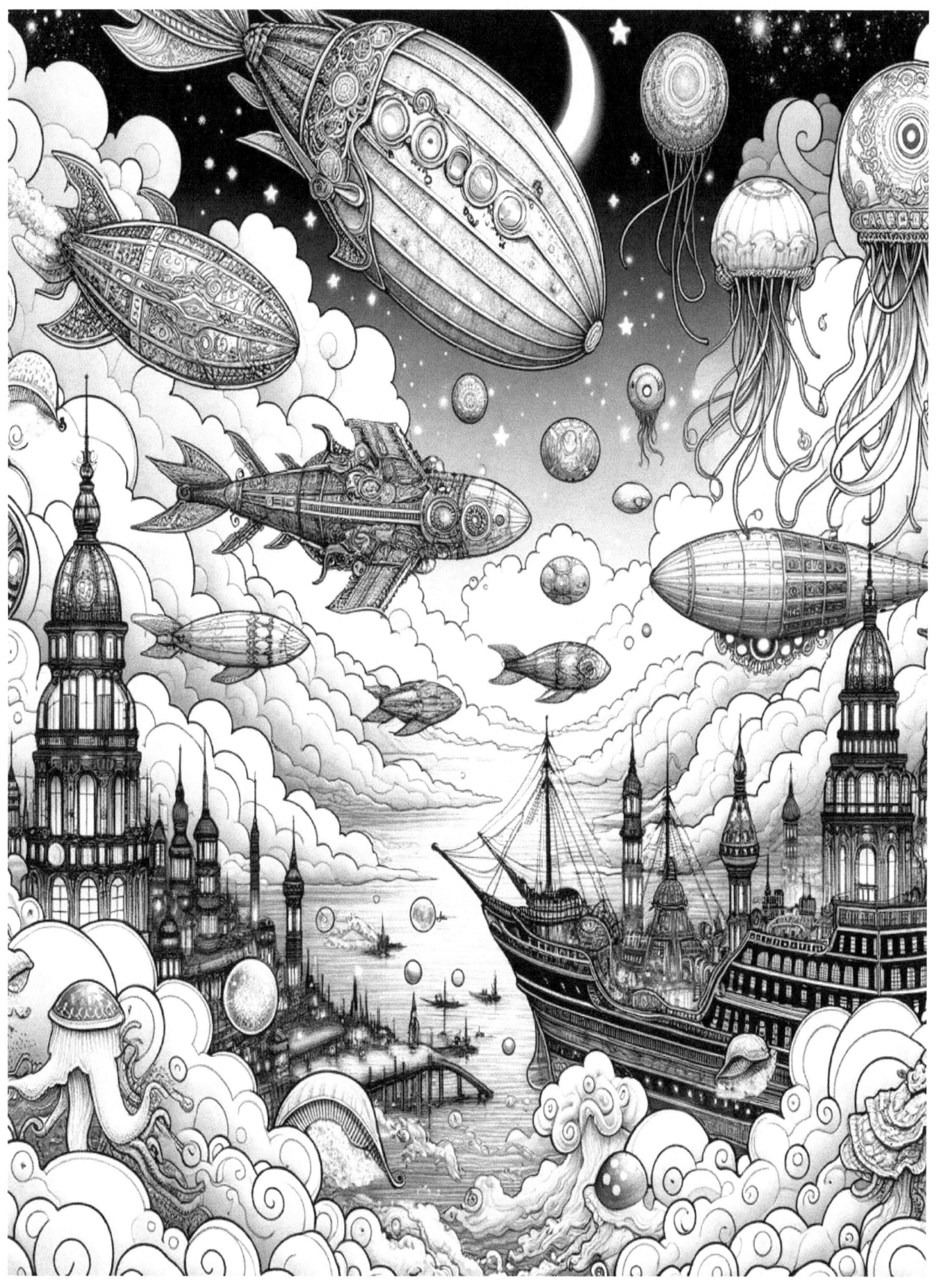

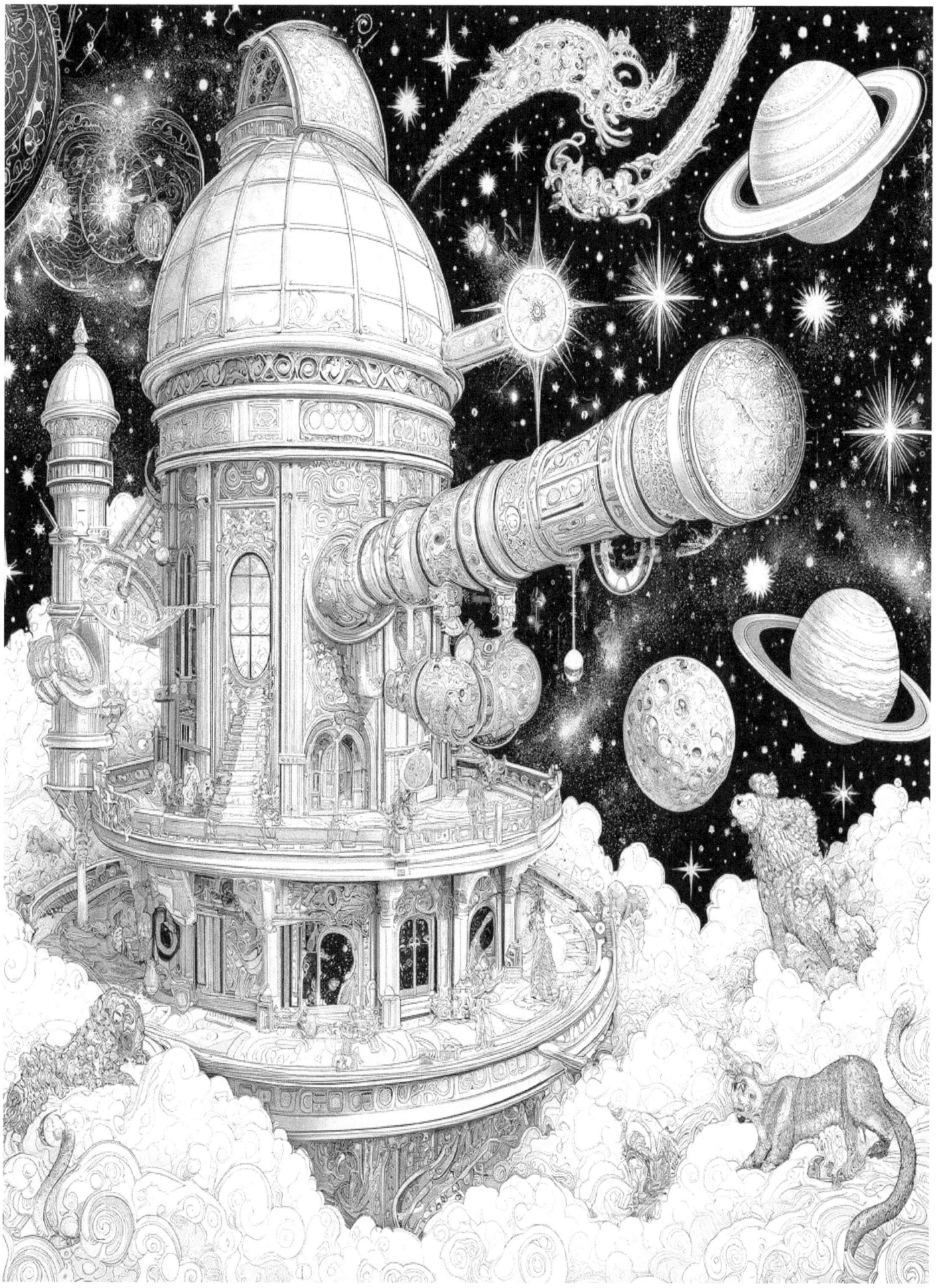

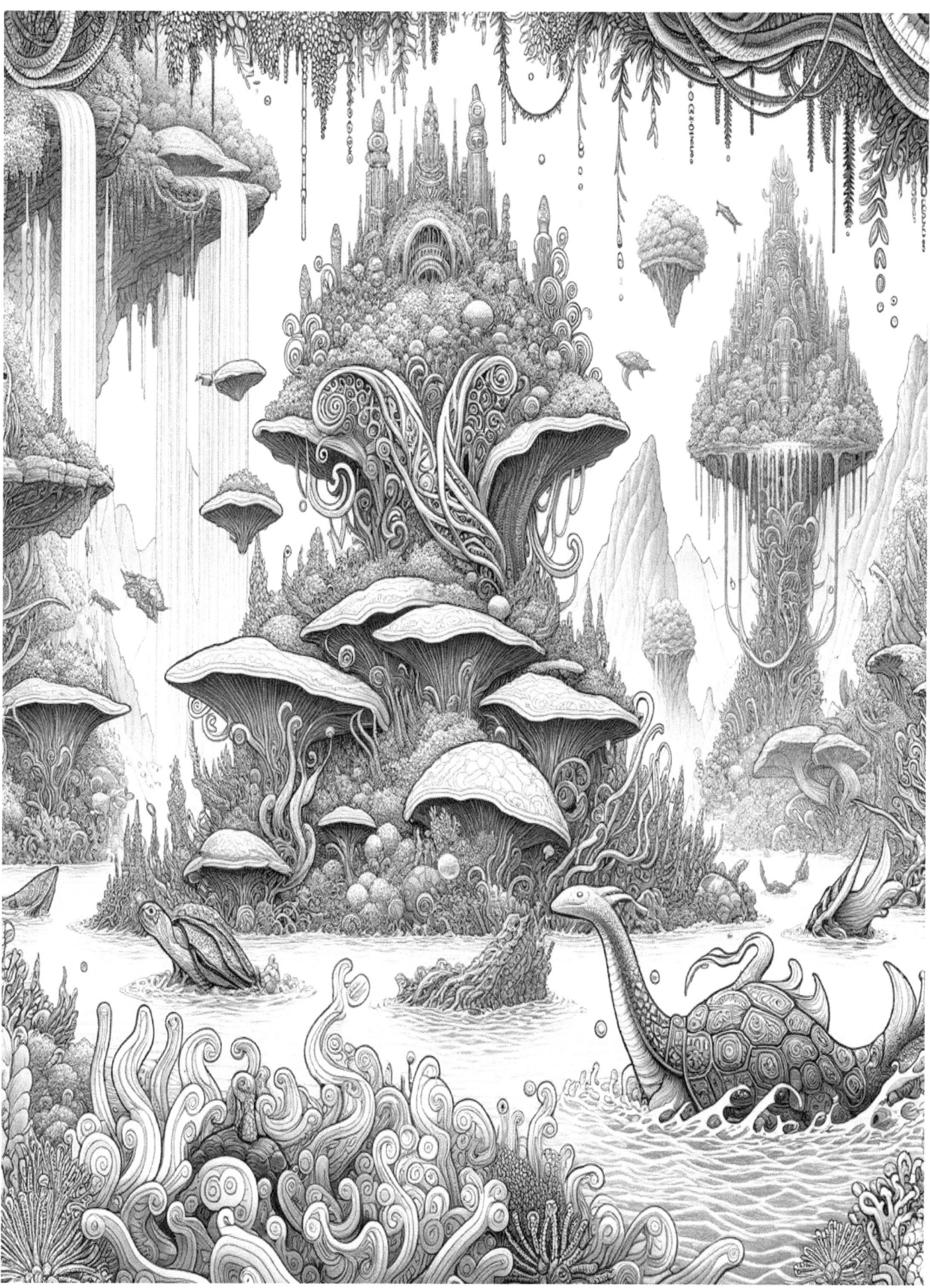

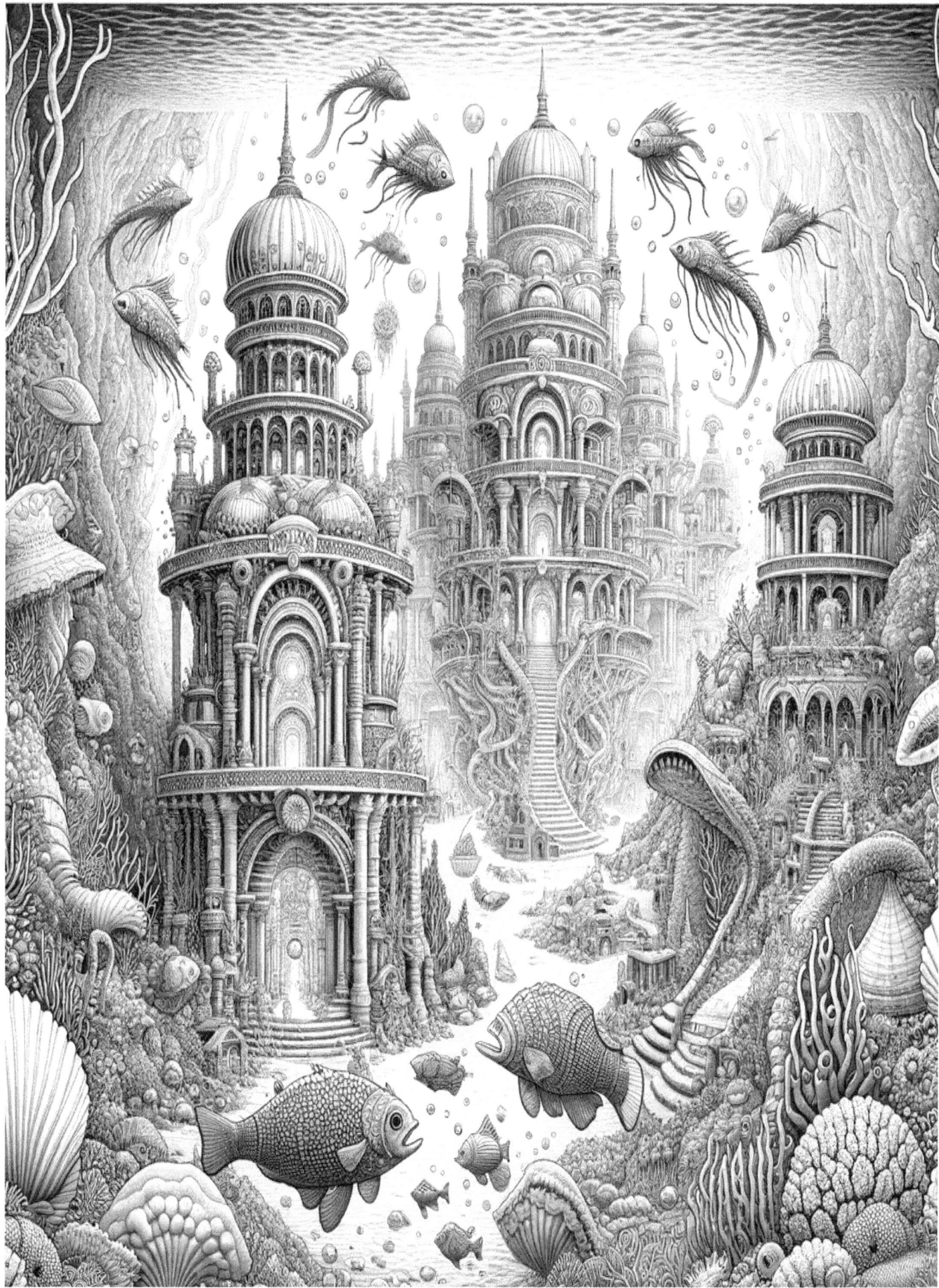

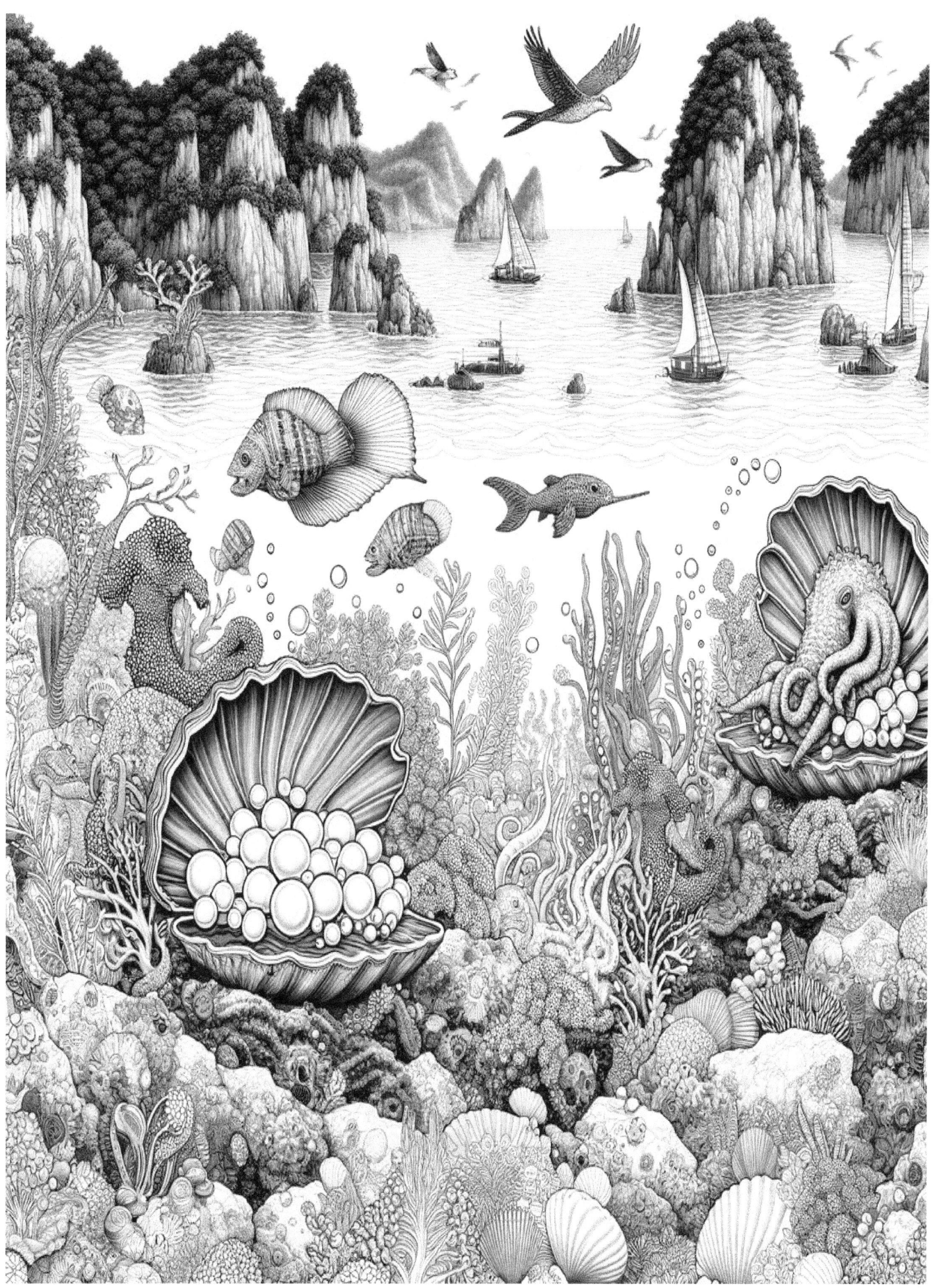

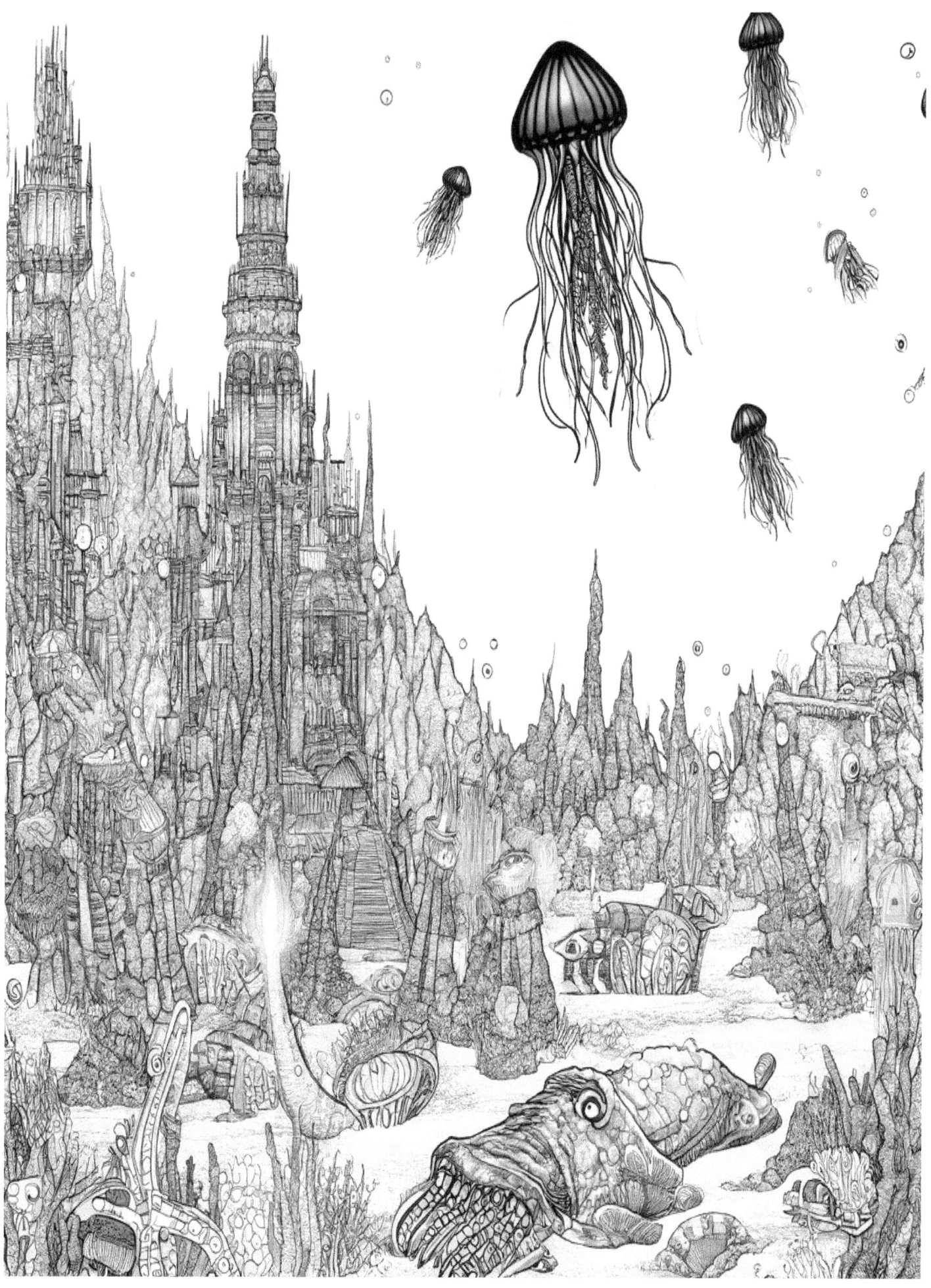

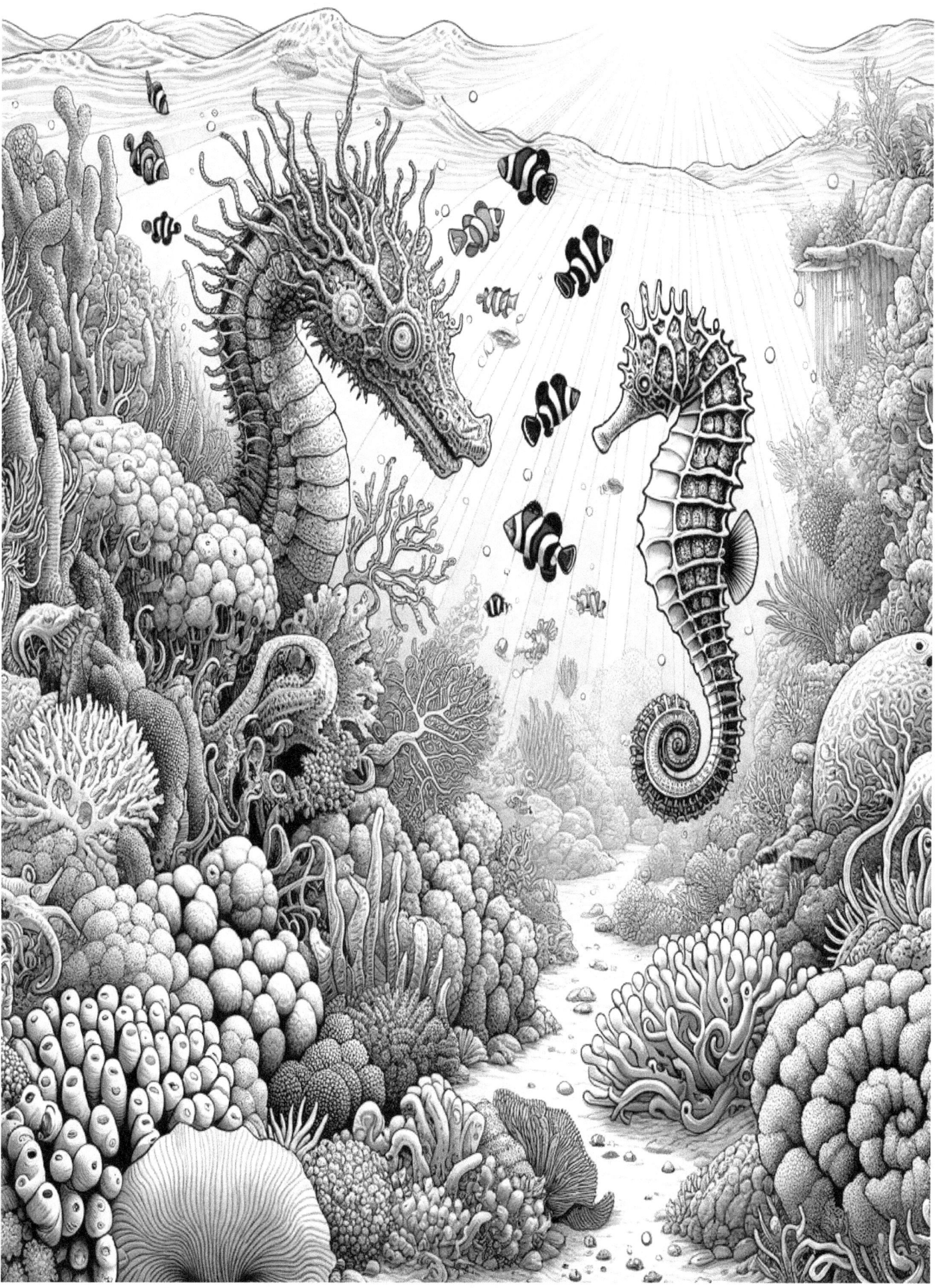

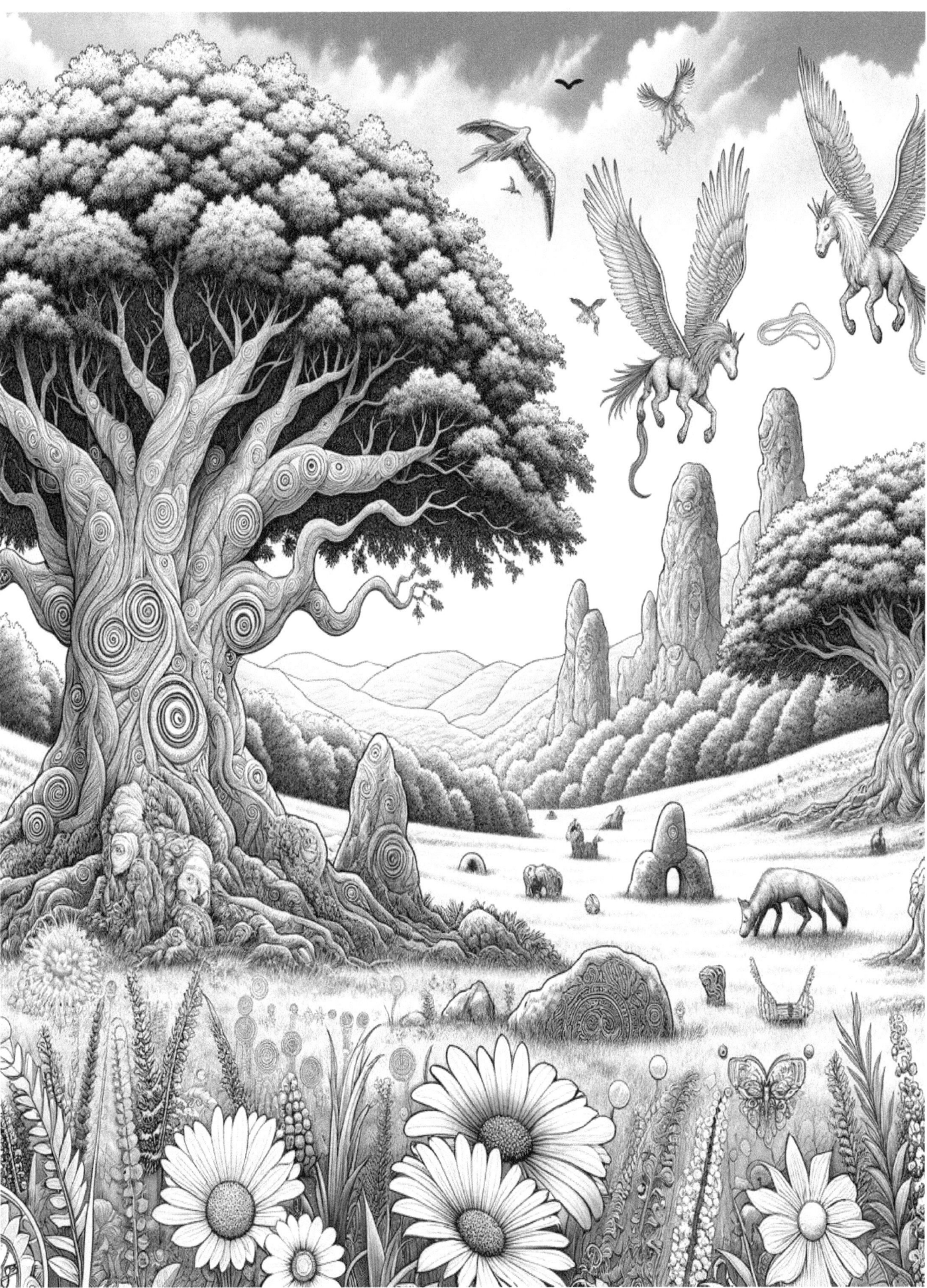

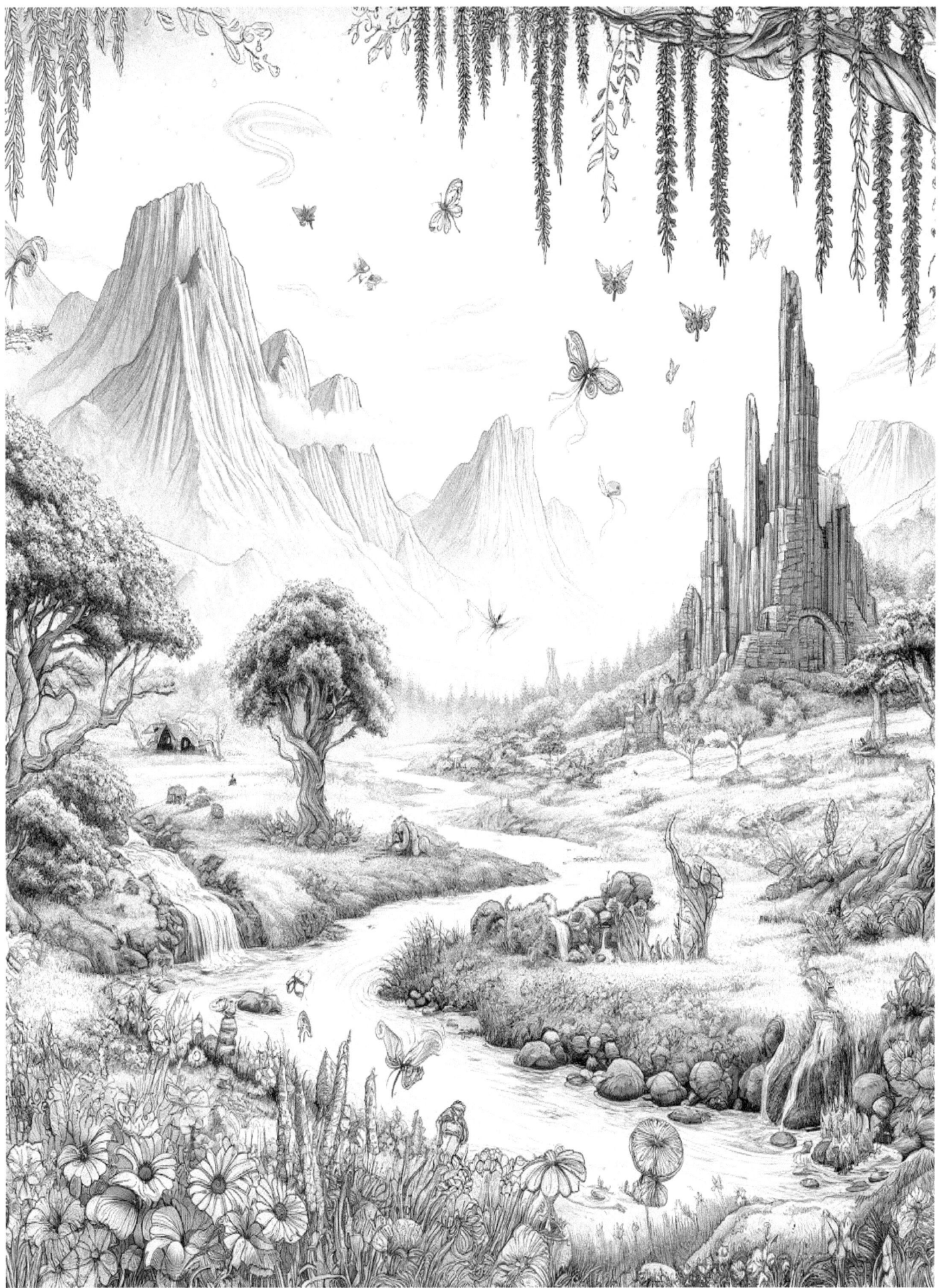

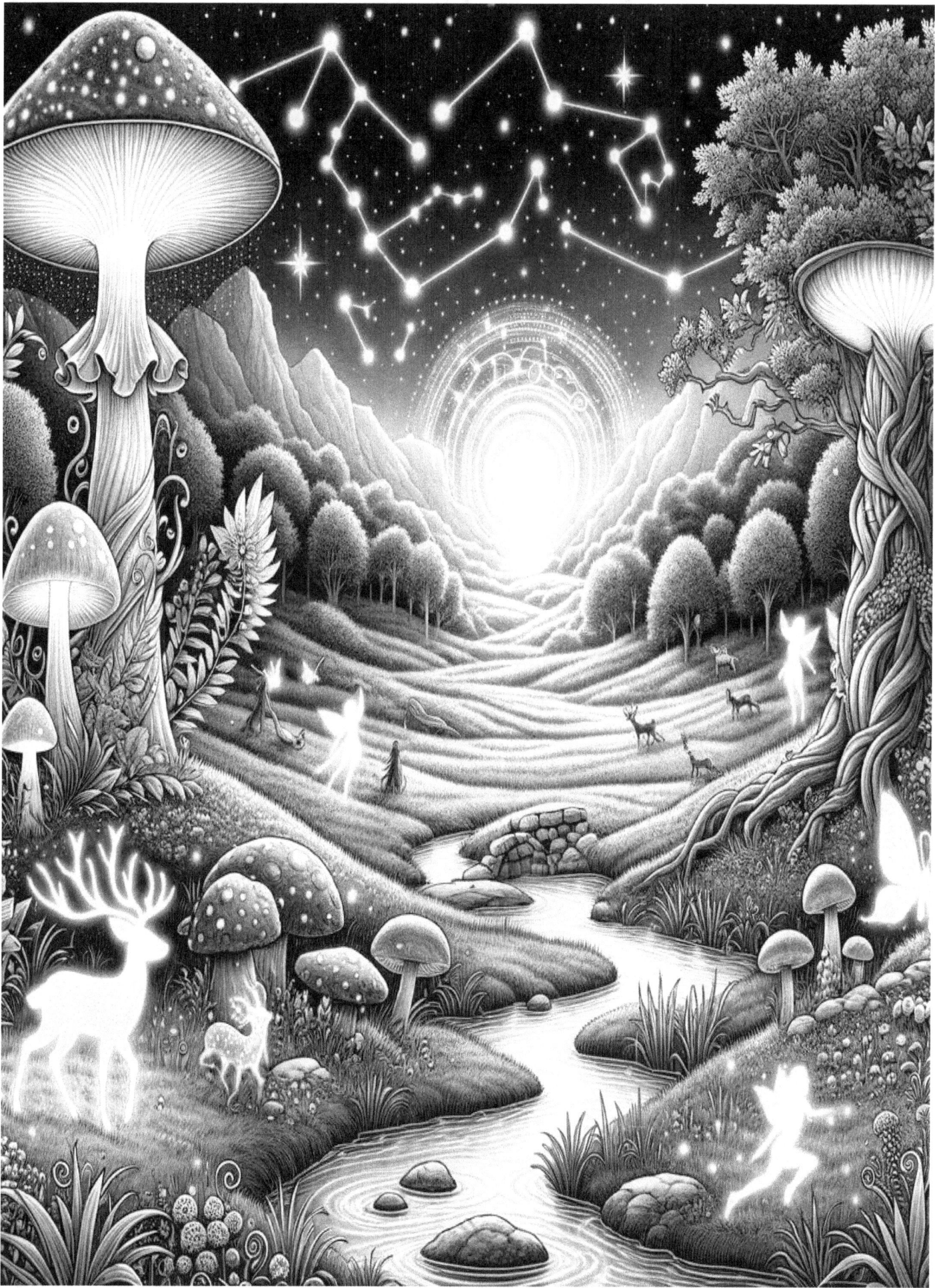

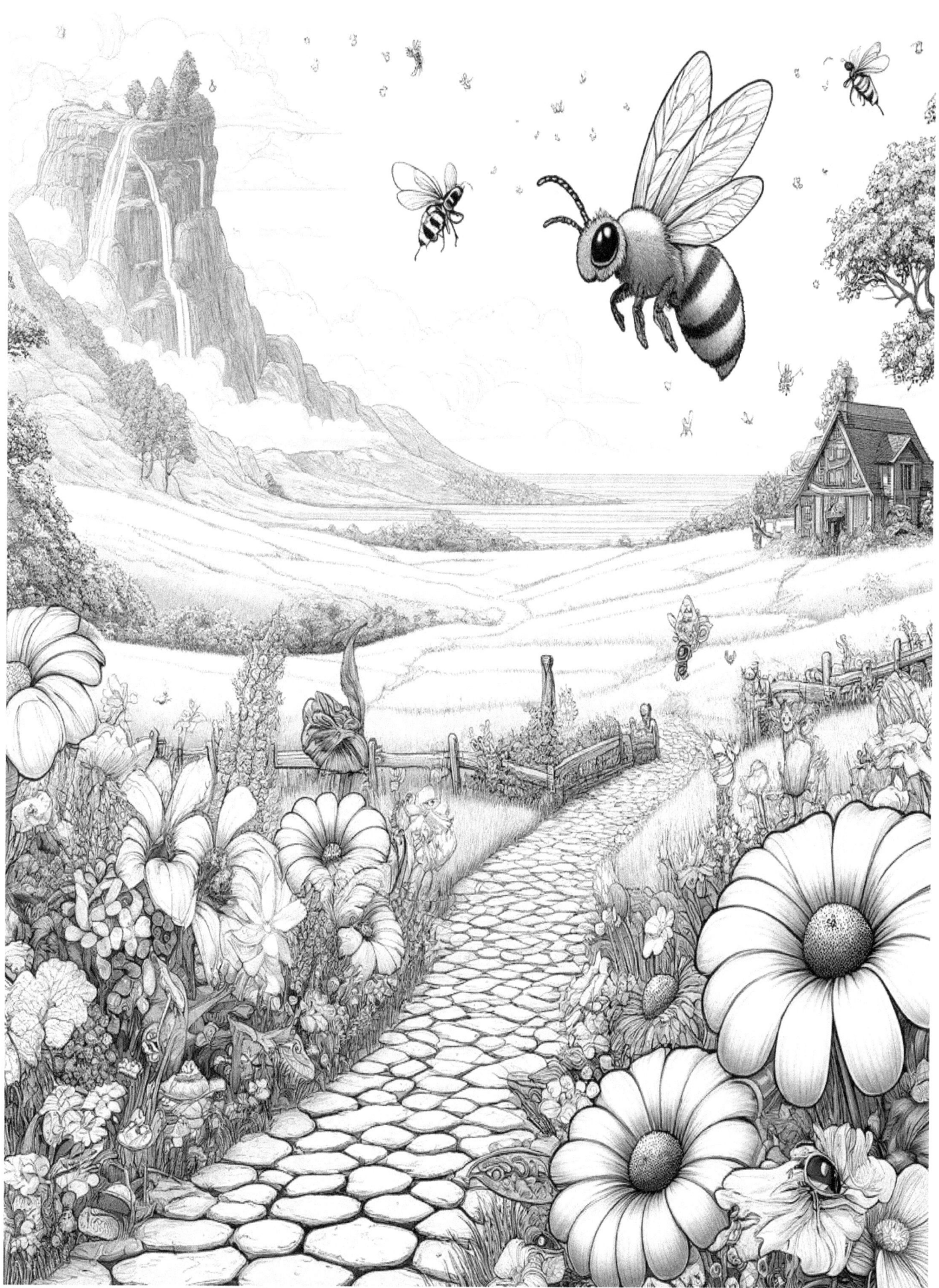

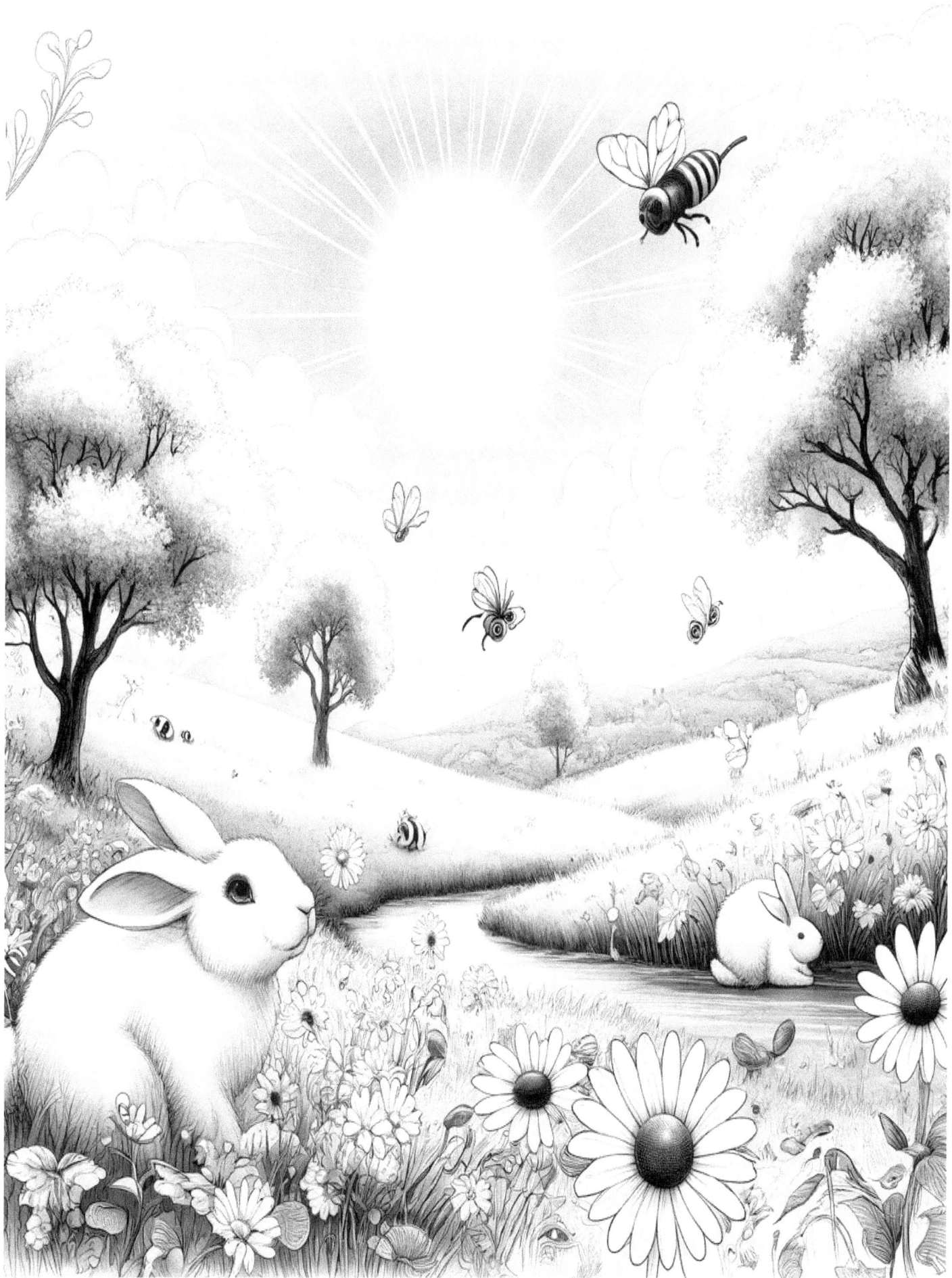

See My Other Coloring Books...

Front

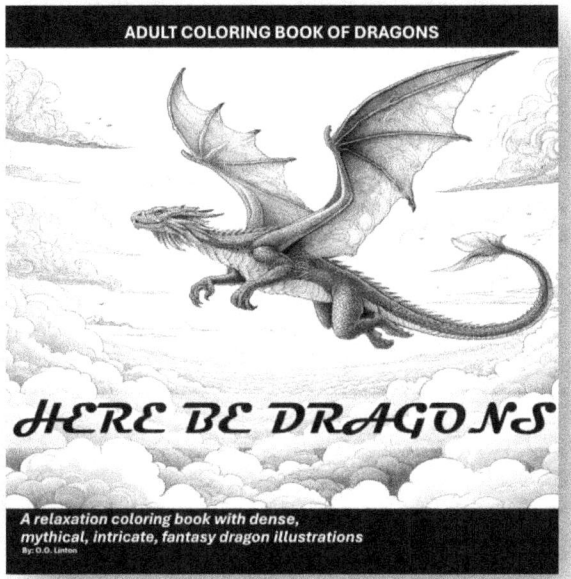

Back

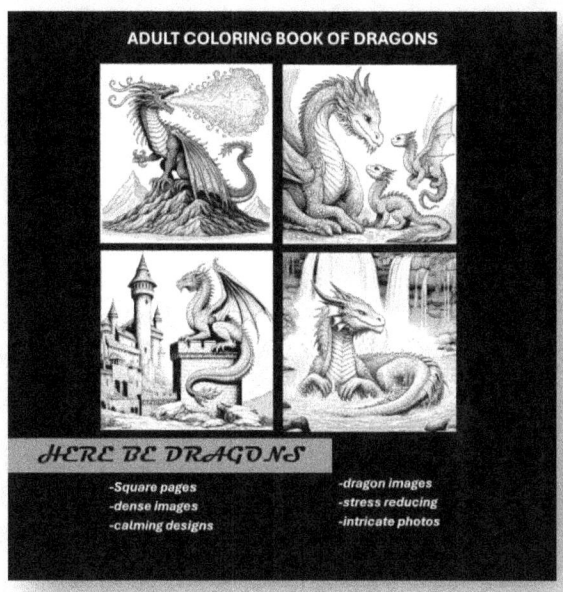

Front

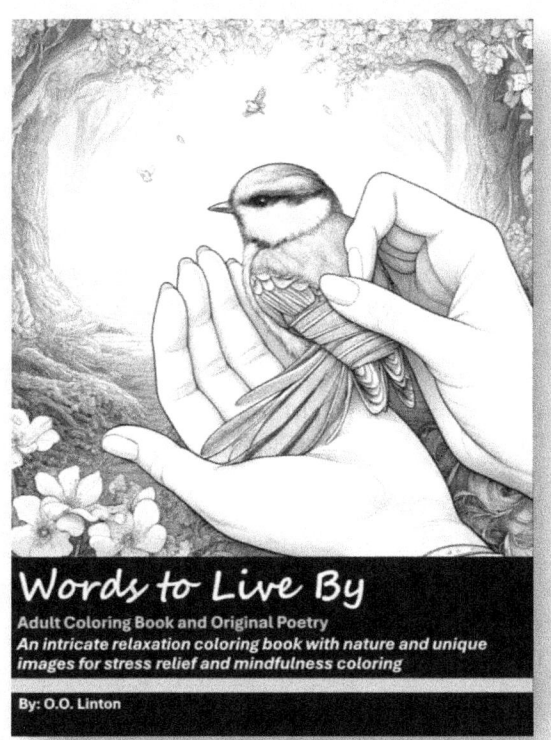

Back

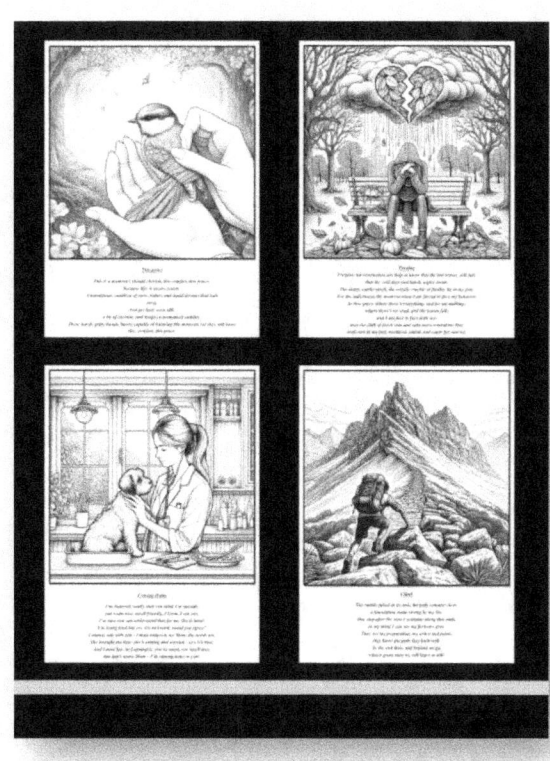

www.ingramcontent.com/pod-product-compliance
Lightning Source LLC
Chambersburg PA
CBHW062235220526
45471CB00009B/3494